We live in a society of patterns and routines, often unaware of the potential threats lurking within these patterns. The top predator on this planet is not one defined by brute strength, but rather by intellect and cunning. Man's mastery of strategy, of premeditation, places him atop the food chain. Yet, this very power can become a double-edged sword, for it requires vigilance and awareness to navigate the complexities of our world. The man-made world, with all its conveniences, can sometimes obscure the primal instincts that lie dormant within us.

Enter The Awareness Formula: A Paradigm Shift in Perception

Consider the essence of predator and prey. Sharks, lions, and bears command respect with their physical prowess, while man's dominance is rooted in an intricate web of intellect and strategy. The formula is simple yet profound: Sight, Hearing, Touch, and Smell, all gateways leading to awareness.

However, mere sensory input is not enough; it's the processing of information, the recognition of threat indicators that unveils the power of this formula.

The brain, likened to a CPU, processes the influx of data. Yet, life's distractions and false senses of security often cloud our ability to assess threats correctly. Anything deviating from the norm must be scrutinized through the lenses of who, what, when, where, why, and how. This is the crux of our pursuit, encapsulated in the phrases "Recognize Threat Indicators" and "Process Information. "In a world where criminal intent often lies concealed, even within our circles, we must wield this formula as a shield. From mundane shopping trips to navigating the complexities of modern relationships, the formula unveils a heightened sense of awareness. No longer shall we be victims—willing or otherwise—of our environment. As we delve further into these pages, we'll traverse areas of concern ranging from commuting to vacationing, from the digital realm to the streets we tread. Through narratives and strategies, we'll uncover the tactics employed by those who seek to exploit our vulnerabilities. We'll explore human trafficking, self-defense, and the intricate stages of grooming used by predators. The road to true awareness is multifaceted, blending the primal with the intellectual, the instinctual with the analytical. The world is not our playground, but a terrain demanding our respect, our vigilance, and our dedication to fostering a society unyielding to those who would prey upon it. Join me on this journey—a journey

Unveiling The Awareness Formula: Rediscovering Our Connection to the Lost Art of Awareness

In a world dominated by the artificial constructs of pop culture, this manual aims to guide you towards reclaiming an intrinsic treasure that has slipped away from our grasp. A treasure known as "awareness," a concept that has been upheld by creatures untouched by the influence of modern media. Imagine a deer, pausing before a sip of water, casting careful glances around, acknowledging the surroundings before quenching its thirst. Or ponder the way the avian world reacts in harmony with nature's cues, dwindling in activity as a storm approaches. Nature's creatures, from the majestic to the minute, are deeply attuned to their environment, a bond severed for humanity by the cacophony of media messages dictating what is good, what is trendy, and what should occupy our thoughts.

Within these pages, we embark on a journey to rekindle the connection we've lost. This lost thing, this "awareness," is not a mere afterthought; it is the key to a life less vulnerable and more in harmony with the world around us. The media, while informative, often cultivates dependency, preventing us from tapping into our own intuition and understanding. It is this reliance on external influences that blurs our ability to recognize subtle signals of danger or sift through information independently.

towards awakening, empowerment, and a safer, more

mindful existence.

This is the beginning of your transformation.

Welcome to "Unveiling The Awareness Formula: Rediscovering Our Connection to the Lost Art of "Awareness."

Key Points of Interest:

Commuting Awareness:

During your commute, observe vehicles trailing behind you. If you notice the same vehicle following you for three or more turns, be vigilant. Make additional turns before concluding your route at the police department. Avoid going near your home, workplace, or neighborhood, as the individual might aim to gather information about you. "Recognize Threat Indicators/Process Information. "Consider how our culture promotes a carefree attitude, akin to a playground mindset. An illustrative example are these ubiquitous bumper stickers.

Both of these aspects provide criminals with valuable insights for planning, particularly if you're driving an upscale or luxury car. Remember that the world isn't your personal playground.

Security Measures for Parking and Returning to Your Vehicle:

- Opt for well-lit, highly visible parking spots.
- Conceal valuables from view.
- Secure all doors and windows.
- Have your keys ready, avoiding fumbling.
- Recognize that criminals seize opportunities.
- Stay cautious of suspicious individuals or cars nearby.
- When unsure, retreat to a store or an area with people.
- Notify authorities of criminal activities.
- "Recognize Threat Indicators/Process Information."

Common Parking Lot Crimes:

- Robberies
- Purse snatchings
- Carjacking
- Abductions
- Rapes

Mass Transit:

Maintain heightened awareness when using mass transit, especially during evening commutes. Attackers find such situations tempting. Everyone reading this guide is advised to invest in personal self-defense tools like pepper spray, stun guns, or self-defense systems. However, a foundation of good awareness remains paramount.

"Recognize Threat Indicators/Process Information."

Home Awareness:

Approaching your home, scan for unusual activity. Have your keys ready for quick entry. Prior to entering, check for signs of forced entry. Lock the door promptly, especially for apartment dwellers. At night, illuminate your surroundings immediately upon entering. Ensure all doors and windows are secure before bedtime. When leaving, use the peephole or window to survey the area. Caution takes precedence over recklessness. "Recognize Threat Indicators/Process Information."

Vacationing Safely:

Tourists are targeted by predators. While vacationing, remain vigilant. Even as you unwind, remember that predators exploit vulnerabilities. Blend in with your surroundings and project confidence. "Recognize Threat Indicators and Process Information."

Safety During Nights out:

Violence can strike anytime, though night hours often see higher statistics. Prioritize recognizing threat indicators and processing information. Designate an awareness person when you anticipate impaired faculties. Remember the principle of a designated driver. Also, be aware of subtle signs, like mind-altering substances.

Social Media Caution:

Approach social media with caution, remembering that the world isn't your private realm. Just as you wouldn't leave your front door open, avoid sharing personal details online. Maintain privacy, even with acquaintances. Not everyone needs to know:

- Where you live
- Details about your car
- Your workplace
- Shopping habits
- Vacation plans
- Home interior
- Family details
- Appearance compliments

Online information lasts, and even seemingly harmless contacts may harbor ulterior motives. Prioritize safety, threat recognition, information processing, and thoughtful

engagement. Don't be swayed by "YOLO" advice;

wisdom outweighs recklessness.

Understanding Human Trafficking:

Forms include:

- Sex trafficking
- Slave labor
- Debt bondage

Sex trafficking coerces victims into commercial sex work.

Slave labor forces victims into various types of work,

from hotels to manufacturing. Debt bondage compels

victims to work to pay off debts, often insurmountable.

Trafficker Tactics:

Traffickers scout locations like bars, malls, and social media platforms. Grooming methods involve kindness, gifts, psychological games, and more. The aim is to gain trust and control.

Stages of Grooming:

- Targeting vulnerable victims.
- Building trust through conversations.
- Addressing victim needs with gifts, potentially leading to Stockholm Syndrome.
- Isolating victims from support networks.
- Exploiting victims through demands for repayment, often involving sex or labor.
- Exerting total control through threats and violence.

Assault Evasion:

Escaping: Against a grab seek always to escape through the thumb, the thumb is the weakest part of the hand. For example if someone grabs your arm don't simply pull your hand up trying to pull it through the thumb area.

You must bend your arm, bringing your hand towards your chest, as you point your elbow towards your opponent. This emphasizes leverage not strength. If someone grabs you around the waist immediately center yourself, by bending your knees, accessing your center of gravity. If grabbed from behind in this position you can fire elbows in a backward motion into the attackers face. If you are grabbed from the front you can use head butts, keep in mind you head butt the middle of the face with your forehead or the back of your head. If someone is much stronger than you, focus on small joint manipulation, like fingers.

Strike Zones: To help you internalize the importance of strike zones when attacked I have provided you with "The Shu Ha Ri Do Self Defense Strike Zone Chart" on the next page.

SELF DEFENSE STRIKE ZONE CHART

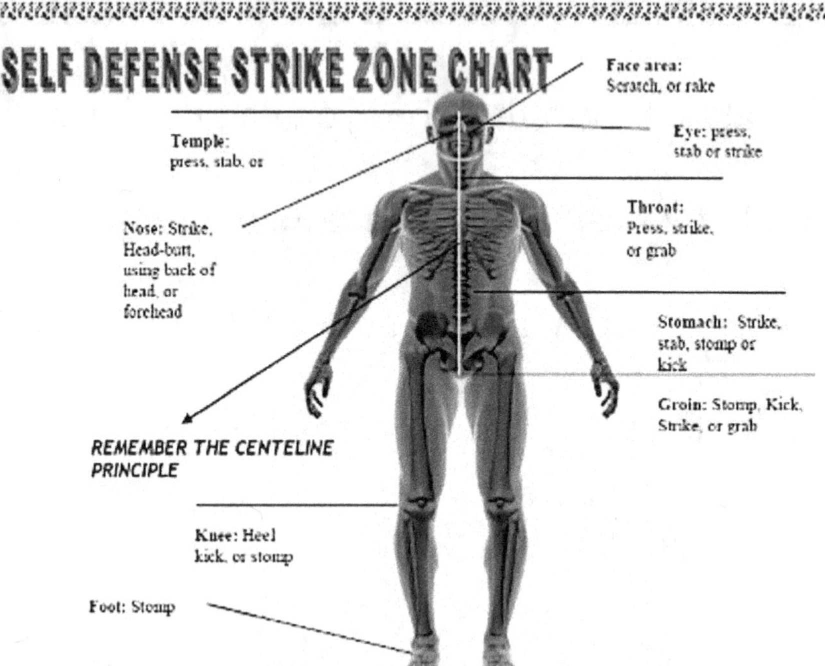

	ROCK	HEADBUTT	FIST	FINGER SCRATCH	GRAB	KNEE	ELBOW	HEEL KICK	STOMP	LIPSTICK TUBE *	KEY *	CELLULAR *	PEN *	BRUSH HANDLE *
Temple		X						X	X	X	X	X	X	X
Face	X	X	X	X		X	X	X	X	X	X	X	X	X
Eyes		X	X	X	X					X	X	X	X	X
Nose	X	X				X	X	X				X		
Throat			X								X		X	
Knees								X						
Feet								X						
Groin			X			X		X						
Stomach			X			X	X	X						

* These are only a few examples of items commonly carried, other items may be used to yield the same result.

As you examine the chart keep in mind the **"Center Line Principle"** which highlights that most vital spots of an attacker are located along the *center line* of the body. These areas are the

- eyes
- nose
- throat
- stomach
- groin

There are many other pressure points and vital areas of course, however, when attacked these are readily accessible. You will notice that included are some areas not found on the center line such as the **knees, temples, &feet**. The knees, and temples although not found on the center line are vita as well. When protecting yourself against an attacker remember these three things

- if they **can't see** they **can't attack**,
- if they **can't breathe** they **can't attack**,
- if they **can't stand** they **can't attack**

The last five items on the chart are examples of common items carried in a purse or pocket. Hold larger items the same as you would a key but with a tighter grip. Place your inner palm at the base of the item using it to drive the item into zone you are attacking. You can use a **pressing**, **stabbing**, or **striking** motion.

Thank you for engaging with "The Awareness Formula." This manual represents just a fraction of the profound Shu Ha Ri Do Philosophy. It merely scratches the surface of what Shu Ha Ri Do training has to offer. To delve deeper into our comprehensive training, please explore www.shuharido.com.

Remember, the true value of knowledge lies in its application. Apply these concepts to your life to cultivate wisdom. Additional works by Sigung G. J. Harris include "Harness the Power Within and Without," "Overcome Mental and Spiritual Manipulation through Self Mastery," and "The Book of Hai/Clue" *Poetic Nuggets of Truth for Seekers of God on the Path of Life*. Stay connected with us at www.shuharido.com for updates. Wishing you a

journey filled with truth, safety, and heightened

awareness. Best of fortune in your quest.

Statutes:

<u>**Sexual Offenders**</u>

<u>**Section 943.0435(12), Florida Statutes states:**</u> *"The Legislature finds that sexual offenders, especially those who have committed their offenses against minors, often pose a high risk of engaging in sexual offenses, even after being released from incarceration or commitment and that protection of the public from sexual offenders is a paramount government interest." One thing to keep in mind is that community notification of a registered sexual offenders is AUTHORIZED it is not MANDATORY.*

Sexual Predators

Section 775.21(3), Florida Statutes states:

"Repeat sexual offenders, sexual offenders w ho use physical violence, and sexual offenders who prey on children are sexual predators who present an extreme threat to the public safety. Sexual predators are extremely likely to use physical violence and to repeat their offenses, and most sexual predators commit many offenses, have many more victims than are ever reported, and are prosecuted for only a fraction of their crimes.

"Unlike sexual offenders community notification of sexual predators is MANDATORY.

Federal Campus Sex Crimes Prevention Act: _"The Campus Sex C rimes Prevention Act provides for the_

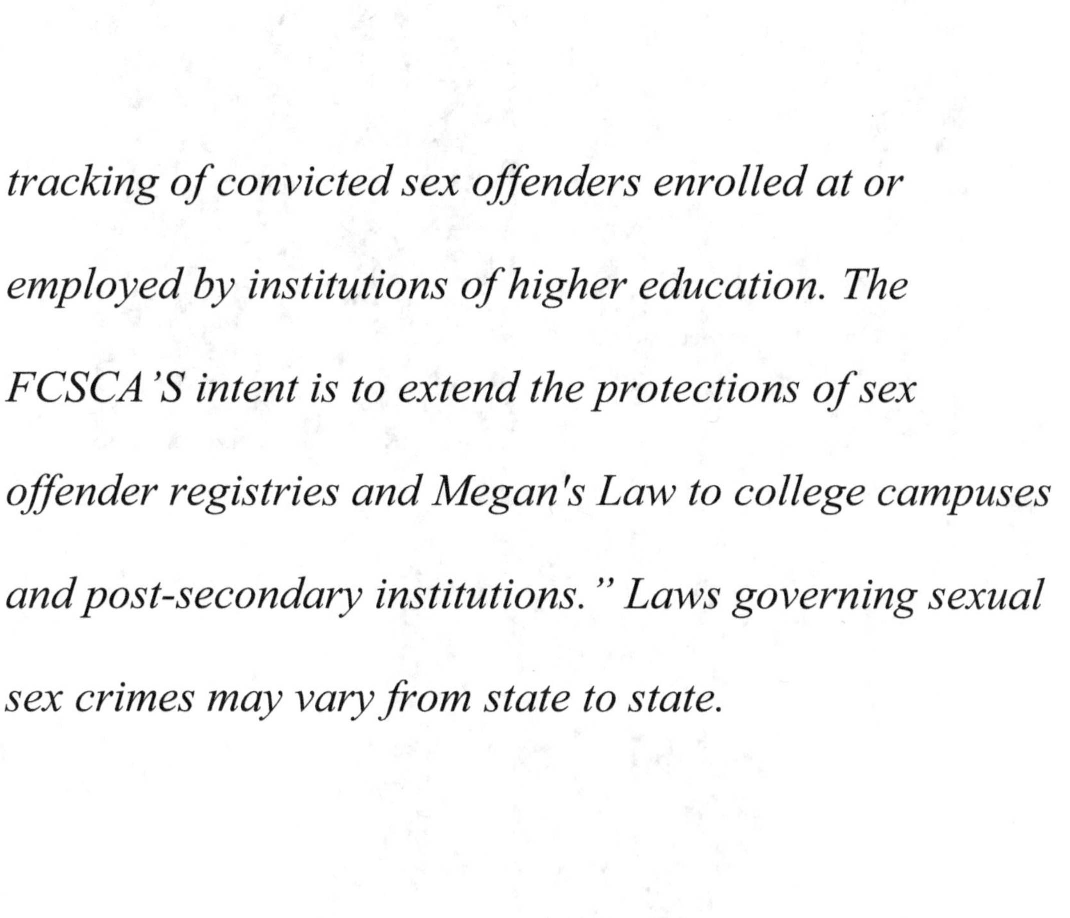

tracking of convicted sex offenders enrolled at or employed by institutions of higher education. The FCSCA'S intent is to extend the protections of sex offender registries and Megan's Law to college campuses and post-secondary institutions." Laws governing sexual sex crimes may vary from state to state.

More books by Sigung G. J. Harris